Industrial Property Investment

I0427516

By

J Cyril

Contents

Value-Add Initiatives

Chapter 1: Introduction to Industrial Property Investment

1.1 What is Industrial Property?

Industrial property refers to real estate properties that are specifically designed and used for industrial purposes. These properties are typically utilized for manufacturing, warehousing, distribution, logistics, research and development, or other industrial activities. They are distinct from commercialor residential properties due to their specialized infrastructure and zoning requirements.

Industrial properties come in various forms, including warehouses, factories, production facilities, storage units, and industrial parks. These properties are often characterized by their large size, high ceilings, heavy-duty infrastructure (such as loading docks and cranes), and proximity to transportation hubs or major highways.

Investing in industrial property offers unique

advantages compared to other types of real estate investments. One key benefit is the potential for high rental yields. Industrial tenants tend to sign long-term leases due to thespecialized nature of their operations and the costs associated with relocating. This stability provides investors with a steady stream of rental income.

Additionally, industrial property has the potential for capital appreciation over time. As demand for industrial space increases due to factors such as e-commerce growth and supply chain optimization, the value of these properties can rise significantly. This presents an opportunity for investors togenerate substantial returns on their investment.

1.2 Why Invest in Industrial Property?

There are several compelling reasons why investing in industrial property can be a lucrative opportunity:

1) High Rental Yields: Industrial properties often offer higher rental yields compared to other types of real estate investments. The demand for industrial space remains strong due to the growth of e-commerce and the need for efficient supply chain management. This translates into attractive rental income potential for investors.

2) Long-Term Stability: Industrial tenants typically sign long-term leases ranging from five to twenty years. This provides investors with a stable income stream over an extended period. Moreover, many industrial leases include rent escalations tied to inflation or market conditions, further enhancing the potential for long-term financial stability.

3) Diversification: Investing in industrial

property allows investors to diversify their real estate portfolio. By adding industrial properties to their holdings, investors can reduce risk by spreading their investments across different asset classes and sectors. This diversification helps protect against market fluctuations and economic downturns.

4) Value-Add Opportunities: Industrial properties often present value-add opportunities that can increase their income potential and overall value. Forexample, investors can renovate or reposition underutilized properties to attract higher-quality tenants or command higher rental rates. These value-add strategies can significantly enhance the return on investment.

5) Favorable Market Conditions: The current market conditions makeinvesting in industrial property particularly attractive. The growth of e-commerce has fueled demand for warehouse and distribution space, while advancements in technology have increased the need for research and development facilities. These trends create a favorable environment for industrial property investment.

1.3 Types of Industrial Properties

Industrial properties encompass a wide range of asset types, each serving different purposes within the industrial sector:

1) Warehouses: Warehouses are large buildings used primarily for storageand distribution purposes. They are typically located near transportation hubs or major highways to facilitate efficient logistics operations. Warehouses come in various sizes, from small-scale storage units to massive fulfillment centers used by e-

commerce giants.

2) Manufacturing Facilities: Manufacturing facilities are designed specifically for production processes, where raw materials are transformed into finished goods. These facilities require specialized infrastructure, suchas assembly lines, heavy machinery, and quality control systems.
Manufacturing facilities can vary greatly in size and complexity depending onthe industry they serve.

3) Logistics Hubs: Logistics hubs play a crucial role in supply chain management by serving as central points for transportation, warehousing,and distribution activities. These hubs are strategically located to optimize the movement of goods between suppliers, manufacturers, and end consumers. They often feature extensive transportation infrastructure, including rail and trucking facilities.

4) Research and Development Centers: Research and development (R&D) centers are dedicated to innovation, product development, and technological advancements. These facilities house laboratories, testing equipment, and specialized workspaces for scientists, engineers, and researchers. R&D centers are commonly found in industries such as pharmaceuticals, biotechnology, and electronics.

5) Industrial Parks: Industrial parks are

planned developments that provide a cluster of industrial properties within a designated area. These parks offer a range of industrial spaces tailored to different needs, including warehouses, manufacturing facilities, offices, and research centers. Industrial parks often provide shared amenities and infrastructure to supportthe operations of multiple businesses.

Understanding the different types of industrial properties is essential for investors to identify opportunities that align with their investment goals and strategies. Each type offers unique advantages and considerations based on factors such as location, tenant demand, market trends, and potential for value appreciation.

By gaining a comprehensive understanding of industrial property types, investors can make informed decisions when selecting assets that best suittheir investment objectives. This knowledge allows them to capitalize on the lucrative opportunities presented by the industrial property market while mitigating risks associated with this specialized asset class.

Chapter 2: Factors Driving Demand for Industrial Space

2.1 E-commerce Growth and its Impact on Industrial Property

E-commerce has experienced explosive growth in recent years, revolutionizing the way people shop and changing consumer expectations. This shift towards online shopping has had a profound impact on the demand for industrial property.

One of the key drivers of this increased demand is the need for efficient and strategically located distribution centers. As e-commerce companies strive to provide fast and reliable delivery services, they require warehousesthat are strategically positioned to reach their customers quickly. These distribution centers act as hubs where products are stored, sorted, and shipped out to customers.

For example, Amazon, the world's largest online retailer, has invested heavily in building a vast network of fulfillment centers across the globe.

These massive warehouses are strategically located near major populationcenters to ensure quick delivery times. The demand for such facilities has skyrocketed as more companies seek to compete with Amazon's speedy delivery service.

Furthermore, the rise of e-commerce has also led to an increase in demand for last-mile delivery facilities. Last-mile delivery refers to the finalleg of the delivery process, from a distribution center to the customer's doorstep.

With consumers expecting faster delivery times, companies arelooking for ways to optimize their last-mile logistics by locating these facilities closer to urban areas.

This increased demand for industrial space driven by e-commerce growth presents lucrative investment opportunities. Investors can capitalize on this trend by acquiring or developing industrial properties that cater specifically toe-commerce companies' needs.

By understanding the unique requirements of these businesses and providing tailored solutions, investors can attract high-quality tenants and achieve attractive rental yields.

Real-world examples highlight the potential profitability of investing in industrial properties influenced by e-commerce growth.

For instance, Prologis Inc., one of the largest owners and operators of logistics real estateglobally, has seen significant success due to its focus on serving e-commerce tenants.

The company strategically acquires land near major transportation hubs and develops state-of-the-art distribution centers that cater to the specific needs of e-commerce companies. This targeted approach has resulted in high occupancy rates and strong rental growth for Prologis.

2.2 Supply Chain Optimization and the Need for Industrial Facilities

Supply chain optimization is a critical factor driving demand for industrial facilities. Companies across various industries are constantly seeking waysto streamline their supply chains, reduce costs, and improve efficiency.

This has led to an increased need for strategically located industrial properties that can support these optimization efforts.

One aspect of supply chain optimization is the consolidation of distribution networks. Companies are looking to centralize their operations by establishing regional distribution centers instead of maintaining multiple smaller facilities. By consolidating their distribution networks, companies canachieve economies of scale, reduce transportation costs, and improve overall efficiency.

This trend towards consolidation has created a demand for larger industrial properties capable of accommodating the increased volume of goods being stored and distributed. Investors who recognize this need cancapitalize on the opportunity by acquiring or developing large-scale warehouses that cater to companies' desire for centralized operations.

Another aspect of supply chain optimization is the implementation of advanced technologies such as automation and robotics. These technologies have the potential to significantly improve operational efficiency by reducing labor costs, increasing productivity, and minimizing errors.

As companies adopt these technologies, they require industrial facilities that can accommodate the installation and operation of automated systems.For example, warehouses need sufficient space for conveyor belts, robotic arms, and other equipment necessary for efficient order fulfillment processes.

Investors who understand the impact of supply chain optimization on industrial property can position themselves ahead of the curve by acquiringor developing properties that are equipped with advanced technology infrastructure. These technologically advanced facilities will be highly soughtafter by companies looking to optimize their supply chains and stay competitive in today's fast-paced business environment.

Real-world examples demonstrate how investors have successfully capitalized on the need for industrial facilities driven by supply chain optimization. For instance, Blackstone Group LP acquired a portfolio oflogistics properties in the United States, Europe, and Asia to meet the growing demand for modern logistics facilities. By focusing on propertiesthat are well-positioned to support supply chain optimization efforts, Blackstone has been able to attract high-quality tenants and achieve strongrental growth.

2.3 Technological Advancements and their Influence on Industrial Property

Technological advancements have had a profound influence on industrial property, transforming the way these properties are designed, operated, andutilized.

From smart buildings to the Internet of Things (IoT), technology is reshaping the industrial property landscape.

One significant technological advancement is the integration of smart building systems. These systems leverage advanced sensors, automation,and data analytics to optimize energy efficiency, improve operational performance, and enhance tenant comfort.

For example, smart lighting systems can automatically adjust lightinglevels based on occupancy or natural light availability, reducing energy consumption. Similarly, HVAC systems equipped with smart controls canoptimize temperature settings based on occupancy patterns and weatherconditions.

Investors who incorporate smart building technologies into their industrialproperties can attract environmentally conscious tenants who value sustainability and cost savings. These technologically advanced properties offer a competitive edge in the market and have the potential for higher rental yields.

Another technological advancement that is

influencing industrial property is the rise of e-commerce automation solutions. As e-commerce continues togrow, companies are investing in automated systems that can handle order fulfillment processes more efficiently.

Automated storage and retrieval systems (AS/RS) are becoming increasingly popular in warehouses as they enable faster order picking and reduce labor costs. These systems use robotic arms or automated guided vehicles (AGVs) to retrieve products from high-density storage racks quickly.

Investors who recognize the impact of automation on industrial propertycan position themselves for success by acquiring or developing properties that are equipped with automation infrastructure. These technologically advanced facilities will be highly sought after by e-commerce companies looking to streamline their operations and improve order fulfillment efficiency.

Real-world examples highlight how technological advancements have influenced industrial property. For instance, Prologis has embraced technology by incorporating smart building systems and automation solutions into its properties.

The company's focus on integrating technologyhas not only attracted high-quality tenants but also improved operational efficiency and reduced energy consumption.

In conclusion, e-commerce growth, supply chain optimization, and technological advancements are key factors driving demand for industrial space. Investors who understand the impact of these factors can capitalize on the opportunities presented by investing in industrial property.

By recognizing the unique needs of e-commerce companies, supporting supply chain optimization efforts, and embracing technological advancements, investors can attract high-quality tenants and achieve attractive rental yields.Industrial property offers a lucrative investment opportunity for those looking to secure long-term financial stability in today's rapidly evolving business landscape.

Chapter 3: Conducting Market Research for Industrial Property Investment

3.1 Understanding Market Trends and Dynamics

Understanding market trends and dynamics is crucial when investing in industrial property. By staying informed about the current state of the market,you can make more informed decisions and identify potential opportunities for growth and profitability.

One important trend to consider is the rise of e-commerce. With theincreasing popularity of online shopping, there has been a significant increase in demand for warehouse and distribution centers. These facilitiesare essential for storing and distributing goods efficiently to meet consumerdemands.

As an investor, you can capitalize on this trend by investing in industrial properties located near major transportation hubs or in areas witha high concentration of e-commerce companies.

Another trend that has shaped the industrial property market is supply chain optimization. Companies are constantly looking for ways to streamlinetheir operations and reduce costs.

This has led to an increased demand for strategically located logistics hubs that can facilitate efficient transportation and distribution of goods. Investing in properties situated near major highways or ports can be a lucrative opportunity as these locations are highly sought after by logistics companies.

Technological advancements have also had a significant impact on the industrial property market. Automation and robotics have revolutionized manufacturing processes, leading to increased demand for modern manufacturing facilities equipped with advanced technology. Investors who recognize this trend can target properties that cater to these needs, such as buildings with high ceilings, ample power supply, and flexible floor plans.

To gain a deeper understanding of market trends and dynamics, it is essential to analyze data and research reports specific to the industrial property sector. For example, examining vacancy rates, rental yields, and absorption rates can provide valuable insights into the overall health of the market. Additionally, studying demographic trends, economic indicators, and government policies can help identify emerging markets or regions with potential for growth.

Real-world examples further illustrate how

market trends impact investment decisions in industrial property. For instance, during the COVID-19 pandemic, there was a surge in demand for cold storage facilities to accommodate the increased need for vaccine storage and distribution. Investors who recognized this trend early on were able to capitalize on theopportunity by acquiring or developing cold storage properties.

In conclusion, understanding market trends and dynamics is crucial wheninvesting in industrial property. By staying informed about emerging trends such as e-commerce growth, supply chain optimization, and technological advancements, investors can identify promising opportunities for long-term profitability.

Analyzing data and research reports specific to the industrial property sector provides valuable insights into market health and potential areas of growth. Real-world examples further highlight how market trends impact investment decisions in this sector.

3.2 Identifying Promising Locations for Investment

Identifying promising locations for investment is a critical step in maximizing returns when investing in industrial property. The location of aproperty plays a significant role in its potential for rental income, capital appreciation, and overall success.

One key factor to consider when evaluating locations is proximity to major transportation hubs. Properties located near airports, seaports, or major highways have a strategic advantage as they provide easy access to transportation networks.

This is particularly important for logistics companies that rely on efficient distribution channels. Investing in properties near these transportation hubs can attract high-quality tenants and ensure a steady stream of rental income.

Another aspect to consider is the availability of skilled labor in the area. Industrial properties often require a workforce with specialized skills, such as technicians or machine operators. Investing in locations with access to a skilled labor pool can make it easier to attract tenants and ensure smooth operations for businesses occupying the property.

Infrastructure development also plays a crucial role in identifying promising locations for investment.

Areas with well-developed infrastructure, including roads, utilities, and telecommunications networks, are more likely to attract businesses looking for convenient and efficient operations.

Additionally, investing in regions where there are plans for future infrastructure improvements can lead to increased property values overtime.

Understanding local zoning regulations and land use policies is essentialwhen evaluating potential locations. Some areas may have restrictions on industrial development or specific zoning requirements that limit the types of businesses that can operate in certain locations. Conducting thorough research on local regulations can help investors avoid costly mistakes and ensure compliance with all legal requirements.

Real-world examples provide further insights into how location impacts investment decisions in industrial property. For instance, investing in properties located near emerging technology clusters or innovation hubs canattract companies seeking proximity to research institutions or other industryleaders. These locations often experience high demand for industrial space due to the presence of innovative businesses.

In conclusion, identifying promising locations for investment is crucial when investing in industrial property. Proximity to major transportation hubs, availability of skilled labor, infrastructure development, and understanding local zoning regulations are key factors to consider when evaluating potential locations. Real-world examples highlight how strategic location choices can attract high-quality tenants and lead to long-term profitability.

3.3 Analyzing Market Demand and Supply

Analyzing market demand and supply is essential for making informed investment decisions in the industrial property sector. Understanding the dynamics between supply and demand can help identify opportunities for growth, assess rental income potential, and mitigate risks associated with oversupply or undersupply.

One way to analyze market demand is by examining vacancy rates. Low vacancy rates indicate strong demand for industrial space, suggesting a favorable market for investors.

Conversely, high vacancy rates may signal oversupply or a lack of demand in a particular area. By monitoring vacancy rates over time, investors can identify trends and make more informed decisions about where to invest.

Another important factor to consider is absorption rates. Absorption refersto the rate at which available industrial space is leased or sold within a givenperiod. High absorption rates indicate strong demand and a healthy market, while low absorption rates may suggest sluggish demand or oversupply.

Analyzing absorption rates can help investors gauge market conditions and identify areas with potential for growth.

Understanding the specific needs of potential tenants is crucial when analyzing market demand. Different industries have unique requirements for industrial space, such as ceiling height, floor load capacity, or access to specialized infrastructure. By identifying the specific demands of target industries, investors can tailor their investment strategies and focus onproperties that meet those requirements.

Analyzing market supply involves assessing the current inventory of industrial properties in a given area. This includes both existing properties and those under development. Understanding the supply side of the market helps investors assess competition and identify areas where there may be ashortage or surplus of industrial space.

Real-world examples further illustrate how analyzing market demand and supply can inform investment decisions. For instance, if there is a high demand for cold storage facilities due to an increase in online grocery shopping, investing in this niche sector can lead to higher rental yields and capital appreciation. On the other hand, investing in an area with an oversupply of generic warehouse space may result in lower rental income and longer vacancy periods.

In conclusion, analyzing market demand and supply is crucial when investing in industrial property. Monitoring vacancy rates, absorption rates, and understanding tenant needs helps investors gauge market conditions and identify areas with growth potential.

Assessing the supply side of the market allows investors to evaluate competition and make informed decisions about where to invest. Real-world examples highlight how analyzing market dynamics can lead to profitable investment opportunities inthe industrial property sector.

Chapter 4: Evaluating Potential Industrial Properties

4.1 Assessing Physical Characteristics of Properties

When evaluating potential industrial properties, it is crucial to thoroughlyassess their physical characteristics. This involves examining various aspects such as location, size, layout, infrastructure, and condition of the property.

One key consideration is the location of the property. Industrial properties that are strategically located in close proximity to major transportation routes, ports, or distribution centers tend to attract higher demand and command higher rental rates. For example, a warehouse located near a major highway, or an airport will have easier access for transportation and logistics purposes.

The size and layout of the property are also important factors to consider. The size should be suitable for the intended use of the property, whether it isfor warehousing, manufacturing, or distribution purposes. Additionally, the layout should be efficient and allow for smooth operations within the facility.For instance, a warehouse with ample space for storage racks and easy maneuverability for forklifts will be more desirable than one with cramped spaces and narrow aisles.

Infrastructure plays a vital role in assessing industrial properties. This includes utilities such as electricity supply, water availability, and internetconnectivity. A property with reliable infrastructure can support various industrial activities without disruptions. Additionally, considering the availability of loading docks, parking spaces, and other amenities can further enhance the functionality of the property.

Another critical aspect is evaluating the condition of the property. Conducting thorough inspections to identify any structural issues or maintenance requirements is essential before making an investment decision. This includes assessing the roof's condition, checking for any signsof water damage or leaks, inspecting electrical systems and plumbing fixtures, and ensuring compliance with safety regulations.

To illustrate these considerations further, let's consider an example.

Imagine you are evaluating two potential industrial properties: Property A is located near a major seaport with excellent road connectivity while Property B is situated in a remote area with limited access to transportation routes.

Property A has a larger size compared to Property B, allowing for more storage capacity and operational flexibility. The layout of Property A is well-designed, with wide aisles and ample space for loading and unloading activities. On the other hand, Property B has a cramped layout, making it challenging to efficiently move goods within the facility.

In terms of infrastructure, Property A has a reliable power supply, high-speed internet connectivity, and sufficient parking spaces for trucks and employees. However, Property B lacks adequate utilities and amenities, which could hinder its functionality.

Lastly, upon inspection, both properties are in good condition overall.
However, Property A requires minor repairs to the roof due to some signs ofwear and tear. In contrast, Property B needs significant renovations to address structural issues and bring it up to code.

By thoroughly assessing these physical characteristics of industrial properties like location, size, layout, infrastructure, and condition, investorscan make informed decisions that align with their investment goals and maximize the potential returns on their investments.

4.1 Analyzing Financial Performance and Potential Returns

Analyzing the financial performance and potential returns of industrial properties is crucial for investors seeking long-term financial stability. This involves evaluating key financial metrics such as rental income, occupancy rates, operating expenses, capitalization rates (cap rates), and potential appreciation.

One of the primary considerations when analyzing financial performanceis rental income. Investors need to assess the current rental rates in the market for similar industrial properties to determine if the property's rental income is competitive or has room for improvement. Additionally, understanding lease terms such as length and escalation clauses canprovide insights into future income growth potential.

Occupancy rates also play a significant role in evaluating financial performance. High occupancy rates indicate strong demand for industrial space in a particular area or property type. Conversely, low occupancy ratesmay signal challenges in attracting tenants or maintaining long-term leases.It is essential to consider historical occupancy trends as well as projected demand in order to estimate future cash flows accurately.

Operating expenses are another critical factor to consider. These include costs such as property taxes, insurance, maintenance, utilities, and propertymanagement fees. Analyzing these expenses in relation to the rental incomecan help determine the property's net operating income (NOI) and its potential profitability. It is important to carefully review historical expense data and consider any potential cost-saving measures or efficiency improvements.

Capitalization rates (cap rates) are widely used in the real estate industryto assess the rate of return on an investment property. Cap rates are calculated by dividing the property's NOI by its purchase price or current market value. Higher cap rates indicate higher potential returns, while lowercap rates suggest lower returns. However, it is crucial to compare cap rateswith similar properties in the market to ensure accurate benchmarking.

In addition to evaluating current financial performance, investors should also consider the potential for appreciation in industrial properties. This can be influenced by factors such as location, market trends, infrastructure development, and overall economic conditions. For example, investing in an industrial property located in an area experiencing significant population growth or infrastructure improvements may lead to increased demand and higher property values over time.

To illustrate these concepts further, let's consider an example. Suppose you are analyzing two industrial properties:

Property X and Property Y.

Property X has a high occupancy rate of 95% due to its prime location near a major logistics hub and strong demand from e-commerce companies.The rental income generated from long-term leases is above market average, providing stable cash flow for investors. Additionally, Property X has relatively low operating expenses compared to similar properties in the area due to efficient management practices.

On the other hand, Property Y has a lower occupancy rate of 80% due toits less desirable location and limited demand from tenants. The rental income generated is below market average but has potential for

improvement through targeted marketing efforts and lease renegotiations.

However, Property Y has higher operating expenses due to its older infrastructure and ongoing maintenance requirements.

These analyses provide insights into the property's profitability and potential returns while considering market conditions and future growth prospects.

4.1 Considering Legal and Regulatory Factors

When evaluating potential industrial properties for investment purposes, it is crucial to consider legal and regulatory factors that may impact the property's operations and profitability. Understanding these factors can helpinvestors mitigate risks and ensure compliance with applicable laws and regulations.

One important legal consideration is zoning regulations. Zoning lawsdictate how land can be used within a specific jurisdiction. Industrial properties are typically zoned for specific uses such as manufacturing, warehousing, or distribution activities. It is essential to review local zoningordinances to ensure that the intended use of the property aligns with its current zoning designation. Additionally, understanding any restrictions or limitations imposed by zoning regulations can help avoid costly violations ordelays in obtaining necessary permits.

Environmental regulations are another critical aspect to consider when evaluating industrial properties. Industrial activities often involve handling hazardous materials or generating waste that must be managed properly to comply with environmental laws. Conducting thorough environmental due diligence assessments can help identify any potential contamination issuesor liabilities associated with the property. This includes reviewing historical site usage, conducting soil and groundwater testing, and assessing compliance with environmental permits and regulations.

Building codes and safety regulations are also important legal factors to consider. Industrial properties must comply with specific building codes to ensure the safety of occupants and protect against potential hazards. It is essential to review the property's compliance with fire safety standards, accessibility requirements, electrical codes, and other relevant regulations. Failure to meet these requirements can result in fines, penalties, or even closure of the facility.

Lease agreements and tenant relationships are additional legal considerations for industrial property investors. Understanding lease terms,rights, and obligations is crucial for maintaining positive tenant relationships and ensuring consistent rental income. Investors should carefully review lease agreements to identify any potential risks or disputes that may arise inthe future. Additionally, considering local tenant laws and regulations can help protect both landlords' and tenants' rights.

To illustrate these legal considerations further, let's consider an example.

Suppose you are evaluating two industrial properties: Property P and Property Q.

Property P is located in an area zoned for light industrial use, allowing for manufacturing activities but prohibiting heavy industrial operations due to noise restrictions imposed by local zoning ordinances. It is crucial to ensurethat any planned manufacturing activities comply with these restrictions to avoid potential violations or complaints from neighboring properties.

Property Q was previously used as a chemical storage facility before being converted into a warehouse space. Conducting thorough environmental due diligence assessments revealed some soil contamination issues resulting from previous chemical spills on the site. It is essential to address these contamination issues through remediation efforts before acquiring the property to avoid potential liability for cleanup costs or legal consequences.

Both properties must comply with building codes and safety regulations.

Property P has recently undergone renovations to upgrade its fire suppression systems and improve accessibility for disabled individuals inaccordance with local building codes. In contrast, Property Q requires significant upgrades to its electrical systems to meet current safety standards.

Lastly, reviewing lease agreements for both properties reveals that Property P has long-term leases with established tenants, providing stablerental income. However, there are some disputes regarding maintenance responsibilities outlined in the lease agreements that need to be resolved. Property Q has shorter-term leases with frequent turnover, requiring more active management and marketing efforts to maintain high occupancy rates.

By considering legal and regulatory factors such as zoning regulations, environmental regulations, building codes and safety regulations, and lease agreements, investors can mitigate risks associated with industrial property investments. Thorough due diligence and compliance with applicable laws and regulations are essential for ensuring the property's operations run smoothly and maximizing its profitability.

Chapter 5: Negotiating Deals in the Industrial Property Market

5.1 Strategies for Effective Negotiations

Negotiating deals in the industrial property market requires a strategic approach to ensure favorable outcomes. While each negotiation is unique,there are several key strategies that can help investors achieve their objectives.

One effective strategy is to gather as much information as possible about the property and its market before entering into negotiations. This includes conducting thorough due diligence, researching comparable properties, and understanding current market trends. Armed with this knowledge, investors can confidently negotiate from a position of strength and make informed decisions.

Another important strategy is to establish clear goals and priorities before entering into negotiations. By identifying what is most important to them – whether it's price, lease terms, or other factors – investors can focus their efforts on achieving those specific objectives. This clarity helps prevent getting side tracked by less significant issues during negotiations.

Flexibility is also crucial in negotiations. It's important for investors to be open to alternative solutions and creative compromises that can benefit bothparties involved.

By being flexible and willing to explore different options, investors can often find mutually beneficial agreements that might not have been initially apparent.

Building rapport and establishing a positive relationship with the other party can also greatly enhance negotiation outcomes. Taking the time to understand the motivations and needs of the other party allows investors totailor their proposals in a way that aligns with those interests. This collaborative approach fosters trust and increases the likelihood of reaching a favorable agreement.

Additionally, it's essential for investors to be patient during negotiations.Rushing or pressuring the other party can lead to suboptimal outcomes or even cause deals to fall through entirely. Taking the time necessary for thorough discussions and careful consideration of all aspects of the deal ensures that both parties feel heard and respected throughout the negotiation process.

Real-world examples illustrate these strategies in action. For instance, consider an investor negotiating a lease agreement for an industrial property. By conducting thorough market research, the investor discovers that similar properties in the area have recently experienced a decrease in rental rates due to increased competition. Armed with this information, the investor enters negotiations with a clear understanding of current market conditions and can negotiate for more favorable lease terms.

In another example, an investor is negotiating the purchase price of an industrial property. The investor establishes clear goals and priorities before entering into negotiations, identifying that securing a lower purchase price istheir primary objective. By remaining flexible and exploring alternative financing options or offering other incentives to the seller, the investor is able to reach a mutually beneficial agreement that satisfies both parties' needs.

By employing these strategies for effective negotiations, investors can navigate the complexities of the industrial property market with confidenceand achieve favorable outcomes that align with their investment goals.

5.1 Key Terms and Conditions in Industrial Property Deals

Understanding key terms and conditions in industrial property deals isessential for investors to protect their interests and ensure successful transactions. These terms cover various aspects of the deal, including purchase agreements, lease agreements, financing arrangements, and more.

One crucial term in industrial property deals is "earnest money." This refers to a deposit made by the buyer as a show of good faith when enteringinto a purchase agreement. The earnest money demonstrates the buyer's commitment to completing the transaction and provides some financial security for the seller. If the buyer fails to fulfill their obligations under the agreement, they may forfeit this deposit.

Another important term is "due diligence."
This refers to the process ofthoroughly
investigating all aspects of a property
before finalizing a deal.due diligence
typically includes reviewing financial
records, inspecting physical structures,
assessing environmental risks, examining
zoning regulations, and evaluating any
legal issues related to the property.
Conducting comprehensive due diligence
helps investors identify potentialrisks or red
flags that could impact their investment
decision.

Lease terms are also critical considerations in
industrial property deals.
Key lease terms include the length of the
lease, rental rates, escalation clauses,
maintenance responsibilities, and renewal
options. Investors should carefully review
these terms to ensure they align with their
investment objectives and provide a favorable
return on investment.

Financing terms are another crucial aspect of

industrial property deals.

These terms outline the conditions under which the investor will secure funding for the purchase or development of the property. Financing terms may include interest rates, repayment schedules, collateral requirements, and any additional fees or charges associated with the loan.

Understandingthese terms is essential for investors to assess the financial viability of their investment and ensure they can meet their financial obligations.

Real-world examples help illustrate the importance of key terms and conditions in industrial property deals. For instance, consider an investor entering into a lease agreement for an industrial property.

By carefully reviewing and negotiating lease terms such as rental rates and escalation clauses, the investor can secure a favorable return on investment and mitigate potential risks associated with fluctuating market conditions.

In another example, an investor is seeking financing for an industrial property acquisition. By thoroughly understanding financing terms such as interest rates and repayment schedules, the investor can accurately assess their ability to meet their financial obligations and determine if the investmentaligns with their long-term financial goals.

By familiarizing themselves with key terms and conditions in industrial property deals, investors can protect their interests, make informed decisions, and maximize their returns on investment.

5.1 Due Diligence Process in Industrial Property Transactions

The due diligence process is a critical step in industrial property transactions that allows investors to thoroughly evaluate a property's suitability before finalizing a deal.

This process involves conducting

comprehensive investigations into various aspects of the property to identify potential risks or issues that could impact its value or future use.

One important aspect of due diligence is reviewing financial records related to the property. This includes examining income statements, balance sheets, rent rolls, tax returns, and any other relevant financial documents.

Analyzing these records helps investors assess the property's financial performance, identify any outstanding debts or liabilities, and determine its income-generating potential.

Physical inspections are also a crucial part of the due diligence process.Investors should conduct thorough inspections of the property's structures,systems, and amenities to identify any maintenance or repair issues.

This includes assessing the condition of

roofs, HVAC systems, electrical wiring, plumbing, and other essential components. Identifying potential maintenance or repair costs allows investors to accurately assess the property's value and factor in these expenses when making investment decisions.

Environmental assessments are another important component of due diligence in industrial property transactions. These assessments evaluatethe presence of hazardous materials, soil contamination, or other environmental risks that could impact the property's value or future use.

Investors should engage qualified professionals to conduct these assessments and ensure compliance with applicable environmental regulations.

Zoning regulations and legal considerations are also critical aspects of due diligence. Investors should review zoning ordinances to understand howthe property can be used and if there are any restrictions or limitations that could affect their intended use.

Additionally, investors should examine any legal issues related to the property, such as pending lawsuits or disputes over ownership rights. Identifying these legal considerations helps investorsassess potential risks and make informed decisions about proceeding with the transaction.

Real-world examples highlight the importance of due diligence in industrial property transactions. For instance, consider an investor conducting due diligence on an industrial property and discovering significant structural issues during a physical inspection.

By uncovering these issues before finalizing the deal, the investor can negotiate for a lower purchase price orrequest repairs from the seller to mitigate potential financial burdens.

In another example, an investor conducting environmental assessments discovers soil contamination on an industrial property they were consideringpurchasing for redevelopment purposes.

This discovery prompts them to reassess their investment decision and explore alternative properties that donot carry similar environmental risks.

By diligently conducting comprehensive due diligence in industrial property transactions, investors can identify potential risks or issues, make informed decisions, and ensure the long-term success of their investments.

Chapter 6: Value-Add Opportunities in Industrial Property Investment

6.1 Renovation Strategies to Enhance Property Value

Renovating industrial properties can be a highly effective strategy for enhancing property value and attracting high-quality tenants. While many investors focus on residential or commercial renovations, the potential forvalue creation in industrial properties is often overlooked.

One renovation strategy that can significantly enhance property value is upgrading the building's infrastructure. This includes improving electrical systems, HVAC systems, plumbing, and fire safety measures. By investingin these upgrades, you not only increase the overall functionality and efficiency of the property but also make it more attractive to potential tenants who prioritize safety and operational reliability.

Another renovation strategy is optimizing the layout and design of the industrial space. This involves reconfiguring floor plans to maximize usable square footage, creating efficient workflows, and incorporating modern design elements.

For example, by removing unnecessary walls or partitions,you can create open-concept spaces that are flexible and adaptable to different tenant needs. Additionally, incorporating sustainable features such as energy-efficient lighting or solar panels can not only reduce operating costs but also appeal to environmentally conscious tenants.

Case Study: XYZ Industrial Park

XYZ Industrial Park was an outdated facility with low occupancy rates due to its outdated infrastructure and inefficient layout. The owners decided to invest in a comprehensive renovation project to enhance its value and attract high-quality tenants

The renovation included upgrading the electrical system to accommodate advanced machinery requirements, installing state-of-the-art HVAC systemsfor temperature control, and implementing a modern fire suppression systemfor enhanced safety. The layout was redesigned to optimize workflow efficiency by creating larger open spaces with clear pathways for material handling equipment.

As a result of these renovations, XYZ Industrial Park experienced a significant increase in demand from high-quality tenants seeking modern facilities with advanced infrastructure. Occupancy rates soared from 50% to 90%, leading to higher rental income and increased property value.

6.2 Repositioning Techniques for Increased Income Potential

Repositioning industrial properties involves transforming underperforming or outdated assets into more desirable and profitable spaces. This strategy can unlock the income potential of a property by attracting higher-paying tenants or expanding its use beyond its original purpose.

One repositioning technique is converting an industrial property into a mixed-use development. By incorporating retail, office, or residential components alongside industrial space, investors can tap into multiple revenue streams and create a vibrant and dynamic environment.

For example, converting an old warehouse into a mixed-use complex with retailshops on the ground floor and office spaces above can attract a diverse range of tenants and increase rental income.

Another repositioning technique is targeting niche markets or specializedindustries. Industrial properties that cater to specific sectors such as biotechnology, pharmaceuticals, or research and development can command higher rental rates due to their unique requirements and limited availability.

By investing in infrastructure upgrades and amenities tailored tothese industries, investors can position their properties as premium spacesfor specialized tenants.

Case Study: ABC Industrial Complex
ABC Industrial Complex was a traditional manufacturing facility that struggled to attract high-quality tenants due to its outdated equipment and lack of modern amenities. The owners decided to reposition the property by targeting the growing e-commerce industry.

They invested in upgrading the facility's electrical capacity to support advanced automation systems, implemented high-speed internet connectivity throughout the complex, and created dedicated loading docksfor efficient logistics operations.

Additionally, they added flexible office spaces within the complex to accommodate e-commerce companies' administrative needs.

As a result of this repositioning strategy, ABC Industrial Complex becamean attractive destination for e-commerce businesses seeking state-of-the-artfacilities tailored to their specific requirements. Rental rates increased significantly, leading to higher income potential for the property.

6.3 Attracting High-Quality Tenants through Value-Add Initiatives

Attracting high-quality tenants is crucial for maximizing rental income andensuring long-term stability in industrial property investments. Value-add initiatives can play a significant role in attracting and retaining desirable tenants who are willing to pay a premium for quality spaces.

One value-add initiative is offering flexible lease terms and customizationoptions. Many industrial tenants have unique operational requirements that may necessitate modifications to the property.

By providing flexible lease terms that allow for alterations or customizations, investors can attract high-quality tenants who value the ability to tailor the space to their specific needs.

Another value-add initiative is providing additional amenities and services that enhance the tenant experience. This can include features such as on- site security, ample parking, access to public transportation, or shared conference rooms and break areas. By offering these amenities, investors can differentiate their properties from competitors and appeal to tenants seeking convenience and added value.

Case Study: DEF Logistics Center

DEF Logistics Center was a newly constructed industrial facility located ina competitive market with several similar properties available for lease. To attract high-quality logistics tenants, the owners implemented various value-add initiatives.

They partnered with a reputable security company to provide 24/7 on-site security personnel and state-of-the-art surveillance systems. Additionally, they created dedicated parking areas for trucks and implemented efficient traffic flow patterns within the complex to facilitate smooth operations.

Furthermore, DEF Logistics Center offered shared conference rooms equipped with modern audiovisual technology for tenant use at no additionalcost. These amenities set DEF Logistics Center apart from other properties in the area, attracting high-quality logistics companies looking for securefacilities with added conveniences.

In conclusion, renovation strategies, repositioning techniques, and value-add initiatives are essential components of maximizing returns in industrial property investment.

By investing in infrastructure upgrades, optimizing layouts, targeting niche markets, offering flexible lease terms, and providing additional amenities, investors can enhance property values, increase income potential, and attract high-quality tenants.

These strategies require careful planning and execution but can yield significant rewards in terms of long-term financial stability and profitability in the industrial property market.

Chapter 7: Redevelopment Projects in the Industrial Property Sector

7.1 Identifying Redevelopment Opportunities in the Market

Identifying redevelopment opportunities in the industrial property marketrequires a keen understanding of market trends, economic indicators, andlocal regulations. While there are various ways to identify these opportunities, it is crucial to focus on areas with high growth potential and demand for industrial space.

One effective method is to analyze demographic and economic data to identify regions experiencing population growth, job creation, and increased consumer spending. These factors often drive demand for industrial properties as businesses expand their operations to meet growing market demands.

For example, if a city is experiencing a surge in e-commerce activity, there may be a need for additional distribution centers or fulfillment warehouses.

Another approach is to monitor government

initiatives and infrastructure projects that can stimulate industrial development.

For instance, if a government announces plans to build a new transportation hub or logistics park in a particular area, it presents an opportunity for redevelopment projects that cater to the needs of businesses operating within those sectors.

Additionally, keeping an eye on changing zoning regulations can help identify areas where industrial properties can be repurposed or redeveloped.For example, if an area previously zoned for manufacturing is rezoned for mixed-use development, there may be potential for converting existing industrial buildings into commercial spaces or residential lofts.

Real-world examples can provide valuable insights into successful redevelopment opportunities. One such example is the transformation of Brooklyn's Navy Yard in New York City. Once a declining shipbuilding facility, it has been revitalized into a thriving industrial park housing various industries such as film production studios, artisanal food manufacturers, and technology companies.

This redevelopment project not only created jobs but also attracted innovative businesses seeking affordable yet well-connected spaces.

In summary, identifying redevelopment opportunities requires analyzing demographic and economic data, monitoring government initiatives and infrastructure projects and staying informed about zoning regulations. By focusing on areas with growth potential and demand for industrial space, investors can uncover lucrative opportunities for redevelopment projects.

7.2 Assessing Feasibility and Risks of Redevelopment Projects

Assessing the feasibility and risks of redevelopment projects in the industrial property sector is crucial to ensure a successful investment. It involves evaluating various factors such as market demand, financial viability, regulatory compliance, and potential risks associated with the project.

One key aspect of assessing feasibility is understanding the market demand for the proposed redevelopment project. Conducting thorough market research helps determine if there is sufficient demand for the type of industrial property being developed.

This includes analyzing vacancy rates,rental rates, and absorption rates in the target market. Additionally, studying industry trends and projections can provide insights into future demand andpotential competition.

Financial viability is another critical factor to consider when assessing a redevelopment project. This involves conducting a detailed financial analysisto determine if the project will generate sufficient returns on investment.

Factors such as construction costs, financing options, projected rental income, operating expenses, and potential tax incentives should be carefullyevaluated. It is essential to consider both short-term profitability and long- term sustainability when assessing financial viability.

Regulatory compliance is also a significant consideration in assessing feasibility. Understanding local zoning regulations, building codes, environmental regulations, and permit requirements ensures that the proposed redevelopment project complies with all necessary legal obligations. Failure to comply with these regulations can lead to delays or even cancellation of the project.

In terms of risk assessment, it is important to identify and mitigate potential risks associated with the redevelopment project. These risks mayinclude construction delays or cost overruns, changes in market conditions that affect rental income or property values, environmental liabilities from previous site usage, or unforeseen challenges during the renovation process.

Conducting thorough due diligence and working closely with experienced professionals such as architects, engineers, contractors, and legal advisors can help identify and mitigate these risks.

A real-world example of successful risk assessment in a redevelopment project is the High Line in New York City. This elevated railway was transformed into a public park, attracting millions of visitors and revitalizing the surrounding neighborhood. However, during the planning phase, extensive risk assessments were conducted to address potential challengessuch as structural integrity, environmental contamination, and community impact. By addressing these risks early on and implementing appropriate mitigation measures, the project was able to proceed smoothly.

In conclusion, assessing feasibility and risks of redevelopment projectsinvolves evaluating market demand, financial viability, regulatory compliance, and potential risks associated with the project.

Thorough market research, financial analysis, understanding of regulations, and risk assessment are essential steps in ensuring a successful redevelopment investment.

7.3 Implementing Successful Redevelopment Strategies

Implementing successful redevelopment Strategies in the industrial property sector requires careful planning, effective execution, and a deep understanding of market dynamics. It involves various stages from conceptualization to completion and requires collaboration with professionals across different disciplines.

One crucial aspect of implementing successful redevelopment strategies is having a clear vision for the project. This includes defining the goals and objectives of the redevelopment project and identifying the target market or tenant profile.

Understanding the needs and preferences of potential tenantshelps shape the design and amenities offered by the redeveloped property.

Effective project management is also essential for successful implementation. This involves coordinating various stakeholders such as architects, engineers, contractors, legal advisors, leasing agents, and property managers. Regular communication and coordination ensure that all aspects of the project are executed efficiently within budgetary constraints.

Adopting sustainable practices can enhance the success of redevelopment projects in today's environmentally conscious world. Incorporating energy-efficient systems, utilizing renewable materials during construction or renovation processes can attract environmentally conscious tenants while reducing operating costs in the long run.

Furthermore, engaging with local communities throughout the redevelopment process can contribute to its success

Building positive relationships with community members through open dialogue and addressing their concerns fosters goodwill towards the project. Additionally,involving local businesses and organizations in the redevelopment project can create opportunities for collaboration and support.

Real-world examples of successful redevelopment strategies include the Meatpacking District in New York City. Once a declining industrial area, it has been transformed into a vibrant neighborhood with high-end retail stores, trendy restaurants, and luxury residential properties. The success of this redevelopment project can be attributed to careful planning, adaptive reuse of existing buildings, and strategic partnerships with local businesses.

In summary, implementing successful redevelopment strategies involves having a clear vision for the project, effective project management, adoptingsustainable practices, and engaging with local communities. By carefully planning each stage of the redevelopment process and collaborating with professionals across different disciplines, investors can maximize the potential of their industrial property investments.

Chapter 8: Lease Negotiations in the Industrial Property Market

8.1 Understanding Lease Structures and Terms

Lease structures and terms play a crucial role in the success of an industrial property investment. Understanding these aspects is essential forinvestors to make informed decisions and maximize their returns. While the reference summary provides a brief overview, let's delve deeper into this topic to gain new insights.

One important aspect of lease structures is the length of the lease term. Inthe industrial property market, leases typically have longer terms compared to other commercial real estate sectors. This is because tenants often require stability and continuity in their operations, which can span several years or even decades. As an investor, it is important to consider the potential risks and benefits associated with longer lease terms. While longerleases provide stability and consistent cash flow, they may also limit your ability to adjust rental rates based on market conditions.

Another key consideration when understanding lease structures is the type of lease agreement used in the industrial property market. The most common types are triple net (NNN) leases and gross leases. In a triple netlease, tenants are responsible for paying not only rent but also additional expenses such as property taxes, insurance, and maintenance costs. This type of lease shifts more financial responsibility onto the tenant, reducing the landlord's expenses and increasing net income. On the other hand, gross leases include all expenses within the rent amount paid by tenants, providing them with greater simplicity and predictability in their monthly payments.

It is also important to understand how rental rates are determined in industrial property leases. Unlike residential or retail properties where rental rates are often based on square footage or square meters alone, industrial properties may have additional factors that influence pricing. For example, properties located near major transportation hubs or with specialized infrastructure may command higher rental rates due to their strategic advantages for tenants logistical operations.

To gain a competitive edge in negotiating favorable lease agreements,investors should consider offering value-add services or amenities to tenants. For instance, providing on-site security, access to advanced technology infrastructure, or flexible lease terms can make a property more attractive to potential tenants. By understanding the specific needs and preferences of industrial tenants, investors can tailor their lease agreementsto meet those requirements and differentiate their properties from competitors.

8.2 Negotiating Favorable Lease Agreements

Negotiating favorable lease agreements is crucial for investors in the industrial property market. While the reference summary acknowledges this importance, let's explore additional strategies and insights that can help investors achieve better outcomes in lease negotiations.

One effective strategy is conducting thorough market research before entering into negotiations. Understanding the current market conditions, rental rates, and vacancy rates in a specific location allows investors to havea realistic assessment of the property's value and negotiate from a position of strength. By being well-informed about comparable properties and recent leasing transactions in the area, investors can justify their proposed rental rates or concessions during negotiations.

Flexibility is another key factor in negotiating favorable lease agreements. Industrial tenants often have unique operational requirements that may change over time. Investors who are willing to accommodate these changing needs by offering flexible lease terms or allowing modifications to the property can attract high-quality tenants and maintain long-term relationships.

This flexibility can also be reflected in rent escalation clauses that allow for periodic adjustments based on market conditions or changes intenant requirements.

In addition to flexibility, it is important for investors to carefully review all aspects of a lease agreement before finalizing it. Paying attention to detailssuch as maintenance responsibilities, repair obligations, insurance requirements, and termination clauses can help avoid potential disputes or financial liabilities down the line. Engaging legal counsel with expertise in commercial real estate leases is highly recommended to ensure that all parties' interests are protected.

Furthermore, building strong relationships with tenants throughout the negotiation process can lead to more favorable outcomes. Taking the time tounderstand their business needs and demonstrating a willingness to work collaboratively can foster trust and goodwill. This can result in tenants being more open to accepting lease terms that are mutually beneficial and fair.

Investors should also consider the potential for value-add opportunitiesduring lease negotiations. For example, if a tenant requires specific improvements or modifications to the property, investors can negotiate thesecosts into the lease agreement. By incorporating these value-add investments into the lease structure, investors can increase the property's overall value and attract higher-quality tenants in the future.

8.3 Managing Tenant Relationships and Lease Renewals

Managing tenant relationships and lease renewals is crucial for maintaining a profitable industrial property portfolio. While the reference summary acknowledges this importance, let's explore additional strategies and insights that can help investors effectively manage tenant relationshipsand maximize lease renewals.

One key aspect of managing tenant relationships is proactive communication. Regularly engaging with tenants to address their concerns, provide updates on property maintenance or improvements, and seek feedback on their experience as a tenant can help build strong rapport. This open line of communication allows investors to promptly address any issuesthat may arise, ensuring tenant satisfaction and reducing turnover rates.

Additionally, investors should prioritize building long-term relationshipswith tenants by offering exceptional customer service. Going above and beyond to meet tenants' needs, such as providing timely responses to maintenance requests or offering flexible solutions when problems arise, cansignificantly enhance tenant satisfaction.

Satisfied tenants are more likely to renew their leases at the end of their term, reducing vacancy rates and ensuring consistent cash flow for investors.

When it comes to lease renewals, proactive planning is essential.

Investors should start engaging with tenants well in advance of their lease expiration dates to discuss renewal options. By initiating these conversations early on, investors have ample time to address any concerns or negotiate new terms that align with both parties' interests.

Offering incentives such as rent discounts or upgrades during lease renewal negotiations can also incentivize tenants to stay longer-term.

Furthermore, conducting regular property inspections allows investors to identify any maintenance or repair needs in a timely manner. By addressing these issues promptly, investors can demonstrate their commitment to maintaining the property's condition and provide tenants with a positive experience.

This proactive approach can significantly increase the likelihood of lease renewals and reduce the risk of tenant dissatisfaction.

In conclusion, understanding lease structures and terms, negotiating favorable lease agreements, and effectively managing tenant relationshipsand lease renewals are critical aspects of success in the industrial property market. By delving deeper into these areas, we have gained new insights that can help investors navigate this complex market and maximize their returns. Through thorough research, flexibility in negotiations, proactive communication, and strategic planning, investors can build profitable industrial property portfolios that provide long-term financial stability.

Chapter 9: Financing Options for Industrial Property Investments

9.1 Traditional Bank Loans for Industrial Property

Traditional bank loans are a common financing option for industrial property investments. These loans are provided by banks and financial institutions and are secured by the property itself. They offer several advantages, such as competitive interest rates, flexible repayment terms,and access to large loan amounts.

One of the main benefits of traditional bank loans is their relatively low interest rates compared to other financing options. Banks typically offer lower rates because they have access to low-cost funds through depositsand other sources. This can significantly reduce the cost of borrowing for investors, allowing them to maximize their returns on investment.

In addition to favorable interest rates,

traditional bank loans also provide flexibility in terms of repayment. Investors can choose from various repayment options, such as fixed-rate or adjustable-rate mortgages, depending on their financial goals and risk tolerance. Fixed-rate mortgages offer stability as the interest rate remains constant throughout the loan term,while adjustable-rate mortgages may provide lower initial rates but can fluctuate over time.

Furthermore, traditional bank loans often allow investors to borrow largeamounts of money, enabling them to finance substantial industrial property acquisitions. This is particularly beneficial for investors looking to expand their portfolio or acquire larger properties that require significant capital investment.

To illustrate the advantages of traditional bank loans for industrial property investments, let's consider a real-world example. Imagine an investor who wants to purchase a warehouse for $2 million.

They approach a bank and secure a loan with

an interest rate of 4% per annum and a loan term of 20 years.

With this loan, the investor can spread out their payments over two decades while benefiting from the income generated by the warehouse during that time. The competitive interest rate ensures that the cost of borrowing remains reasonable, allowing the investor to generate positive cash flow from rental income.

However, it's important to note that obtaining a traditional bank loan for industrial property investments may require meeting certain eligibility criteriaset by the lender. These criteria typically include factors such as the investor's creditworthiness, income stability, and the property's value and potential for generating income.

In summary, traditional bank loans offer attractive financing options for industrial property investments. They provide competitive interest rates, flexible repayment terms, and access to large loan amounts.

By leveraging these loans, investors can acquire industrial properties while minimizing theirborrowing costs and maximizing their returns on investment.

9.2 Exploring Alternative Financing Methods

While traditional bank loans are a popular choice for financing industrial property investments, there are also alternative methods worth exploring. These alternative financing options can provide additional flexibility and opportunities for investors to secure funding for their projects.

One alternative financing method is crowdfunding. Crowdfunding platforms allow multiple investors to pool their resources together to fund a specific project or investment opportunity. This method has gained popularityin recent years due to its ability to connect investors with real estate projects that may not be accessible through traditional channels.

Crowdfunding offers several advantages for industrial property investments. Firstly, it provides access to a larger pool of potential investors who may be interested in participating in the project. This can increase the chances of securing funding, especially for investors who may have difficulty obtaining traditional bank loans due to strict eligibility criteria.

Secondly, crowdfunding allows investors to diversify their sources of capital by tapping into a network of individuals who are willing to invest smaller amounts of money. This can reduce reliance on a single lender orfinancial institution and spread the risk among multiple stakeholders.

To illustrate the benefits of crowdfunding for industrial property investments, let's consider an example. Imagine an investor wants to raise $1 million to develop a logistics hub but is unable to secure a traditional bank loan due to limited credit history. By utilizing a crowdfunding platform, they can attract multiple individual investors who contribute smaller amountstowards the project.

This not only provides the necessary funds but also creates a network of stakeholders who have an interest in the success of the project. The investorcan leverage the expertise and connections of these investors to enhance the development process and increase the chances of a successful outcome.

Another alternative financing method worth exploring is private lending.
Private lenders, also known as hard money lenders, are individuals or companies that provide loans based on the value of the property rather than the borrower's creditworthiness. These lenders often offer faster approval processes and more flexible terms compared to traditional banks.

Private lending can be particularly useful for investors who need quick access to capital or have difficulty meeting the strict eligibility criteria set bytraditional banks. However, it's important to note that private loans typically come with higher interest rates and fees due to the increased risk taken onby the lender.

In conclusion, exploring alternative financing

methods can provide additional flexibility and opportunities for industrial property investments. Crowdfunding platforms allow investors to tap into a larger pool of potential funders, while private lending offers faster approval processes and more flexible terms. By considering these alternative options, investors can securefunding for their projects and take advantage of unique opportunities in the industrial property market.

9.3 Real Estate Investment Trusts (REITs) for Industrial Property

Real Estate Investment Trusts (REITs) are another financing option specifically tailored for industrial property investments. REITs are companies that own, operate, or finance income-generating real estate properties. Theyallow individual investors to invest in a diversified portfolio of properties without directly owning them.

Investing in REITs offers several advantages for industrial property investors. Firstly, it provides access to a professionally managed portfolio of industrial properties that may be difficult or costly to acquire individually. This allows investors to benefit from economies of scale and diversification across different locations and types of industrial properties.

Secondly, investing in REITs offers liquidity compared to direct ownership of industrial properties. REIT shares can be bought or sold on stock exchanges like any other publicly traded company, providing investors withthe flexibility to enter or exit their investment positions easily.

Furthermore, REITs are required by law to distribute a significant portion of their taxable income as dividends to shareholders. This can provide investors with a steady stream of passive income, making REITs an attractive option for those seeking regular cash flow from their industrial property investments.

To illustrate the benefits of investing in REITs for industrial property, let'sconsider a real-world example. Imagine an investor

wants exposure to the industrial property market but does not have the capital or expertise to
acquire and manage properties directly. By investing in an industrial-focused REIT, they can gain exposure to a diversified portfolio of warehouses, distribution centers, and manufacturing facilities.

The investor can benefit from professional management and expertise in selecting and managing these properties while enjoying regular dividend payments generated by the rental income. Additionally, they can easily buy or sell shares in the REIT if they decide to adjust their investment strategy orneed liquidity.

However, it's important to note that investing in REITs also comes with certain risks. The performance of REITs is influenced by factors such as interest rates, economic conditions, and property market trends. Investors should carefully evaluate the track record and financial health of the REIT before making any investment decisions.

In summary, Real Estate Investment Trusts (REITs) offer a unique financing option for industrial property investments. They provide access to professionally managed portfolios of industrial properties, offer liquidity through publicly traded shares, and generate regular dividend income for investors. By investing in REITs, individuals can gain exposure to the industrial property market without directly owning or managing properties themselves.

Chapter 10: Case Studies of Successful Industrial Property Investors

10.1 Lessons from Successful Industrial Property Investors

Investing in industrial property can be a lucrative venture, but it requires knowledge and expertise to achieve success. Learning from the experiencesof successful investors can provide valuable insights and lessons that can be applied to your own investment journey.

One important lesson from successful industrial property investors is the importance of conducting thorough market research. Before making any investment decisions, it is crucial to understand the current market conditions, trends, and potential risks.

This includes analyzing supply and demand dynamics, vacancy rates, rental yields, and economic indicators that may impact the industrial property market.

For example, let's consider the case of John, a successful industrialproperty investor who achieved impressive returns by investing in warehouses located near major transportation hubs.

Through extensive market research, John identified a growing trend of e-commerce companiesexpanding their distribution networks. He recognized the need for strategically located warehouses to cater to this demand and capitalized onthis opportunity by acquiring properties in prime locations.

Another lesson from successful investors is the importance of building a strong network within the industry. Networking allows you to connect with other professionals such as brokers, property managers, lenders, and fellow investors who can provide valuable insights and opportunities.

By attending industry events, joining real estate associations or online forums, you can gain access to a wealth of knowledge and potential partnerships.

Consider the example of Sarah, an experienced industrial property investor who attributes her success to her extensive network. Sarah regularly attends real estate conferences where she has built relationships with brokers specializing in industrial properties.

Through these connections, she has been able to access off-market deals and secure favorable terms onher investments.

Successful investors also emphasize the significance of due diligence when evaluating potential properties. This involves thoroughly assessing factors such as location, condition of the property, tenant quality, lease terms, and potential for value-add opportunities.

Conducting site visits and engaging professionals like inspectors or appraisers can help uncover any hidden issues or risks associated with the property.

Take the case of Michael, a seasoned industrial property investor who achieved impressive returns by identifying undervalued properties with potential for redevelopment. Through meticulous due diligence, he discovered an old manufacturing facility in a prime location that could be repurposed into a modern logistics hub. By investing in renovations and repositioning strategies, Michael was able to attract high-quality tenants andsignificantly increase the property's value.

In summary, successful industrial property investors emphasize the importance of thorough market research, building a strong network, and conducting diligent due diligence. These lessons provide valuable insights into how to identify lucrative investment opportunities and mitigate risks. By learning from their experiences, you can enhance your own investment journey and increase your chances of achieving impressive returns.

10.1 Strategies and Tactics for Achieving Impressive Returns

Achieving impressive returns in industrial

property investment requiresstrategic planning and tactical execution. Successful investors employ various strategies to maximize their profits while minimizing risks.

Understanding these strategies can help you develop your own approach toinvesting in industrial property. One strategy commonly used by successful investors is focusing on specific submarkets or niche sectors within the industrial property market. Instead of spreading their investments across different types of properties, they concentrate on areas where they have expertise or see significant growth potential.

For example, consider the case of Lisa, a successful investor who specializes in investing in cold storage facilities.

She recognized the increasing demand for temperature-controlled warehouses due to the growth of online grocery shopping and food delivery services. By focusing exclusively on this niche sector, Lisa was able to capitalize on the limited supply of such facilities and achieve impressive rental yields.

Another strategy employed by successful investors is value-add investing. This involves identifying underperforming or distressed properties with potential for improvement and implementing strategies to enhance their value.

Value-add opportunities can include renovations, repositioning, lease negotiations, or attracting higher-quality tenants.

Let's look at the example of David, an experienced industrial property investor who achieved impressive returns by implementing value-add strategies.

David identified an older warehouse with outdated amenities andlow occupancy rates. He saw the potential to increase the property's value by renovating the interior, upgrading the HVAC system, and improving the overall aesthetics.

By investing in these improvements, David was able to attract higher-quality tenants and significantly increase rental income.

Successful investors also employ financing strategies to optimize their returns. They explore various funding options such as traditional bank loans,private lenders, real estate investment trusts (REITs), or even crowdfunding platforms.

By carefully evaluating the costs and terms associated with each financing option, investors can choose the most suitable solution for their specific investment goals.

Consider the case of Mark, a successful industrial property investor who utilized crowdfunding to finance his investments. Mark recognized that traditional bank loans were becoming increasingly difficult to obtain due to stricter lending criteria.

Instead of giving up on his investment plans, he turned to crowdfunding platforms that allowed him to pool funds from multiple investors. This alternative financing method enabled Mark to securecapital for his projects while offering attractive returns to his investors.

In summary, achieving impressive returns in industrial property investmentrequires strategic planning and tactical execution. Successful investors employ strategies such as focusing on niche sectors, implementing value- add opportunities, and exploring various financing options.

By adopting these strategies and tailoring them to your own investment goals, you can increase your chances of achieving impressive returns in this lucrative asset class.

10.2 Applying Real-Life Examples to Your Own Investment Journey

Real-life examples from successful industrial property investors serve as valuable sources of inspiration and practical insights that can be applied toyour own investment journey.

Analyzing these examples can help you understand how successful investors identify opportunities, overcome challenges, and achieve impressive returns.

One key lesson from real-life examples is the importance of adapting tomarket trends and technological advancements. Successful investors stay informed about emerging trends that impact the industrial property marketand adjust their investment strategies accordingly.

For instance, let's consider the case of Alex, a successful investor who recognized the growing demand for last-mile distribution centers due to therise of e-commerce. He studied consumer behavior and identified key locations where these facilities would be in high demand. By investing in strategically located properties near urban centers, Alex was able to attract major e-commerce companies as tenants and achieve impressive rental yields.

Real-life examples also highlight the significance of building a team of professionals to support your investment journey. Successful investors surround themselves with experts such as real estate agents, property managers, lawyers, and accountants who can provide valuable advice and guidance.

Take the example of Emily, a successful industrial property investor who attributes her success to her team of professionals. She works closely with a trusted real estate agent who specializes in industrial properties and has extensive knowledge of the local market. This partnership has allowed Emily to access off-market deals and negotiate favorable terms on her investments.

Furthermore, real-life examples demonstrate the importance of patience and long-term thinking in industrial property investment. Successful investors understand that building a profitable portfolio takes time andrequires careful planning.

Consider the case of Robert, an experienced investor who started small by acquiring a single warehouse property. Over time, he gradually expandedhis portfolio by reinvesting profits into new acquisitions. Through disciplined investing and strategic decision-making, Robert was able to build a diverse portfolio of industrial properties that generated impressive returns over the years.

In summary, real-life examples from successful industrial property investors offer valuable insights that can be applied to your own investmentjourney. They emphasize the importance of adapting to market trends, building a team of professionals, and adopting a patient long-term approach. By studying these examples and incorporating their lessons into your own strategy, you can increase your chances of achieving success in industrial property investment.

Chapter 11: Actionable Advice, Checklists, and Resources

11.1 Practical Steps for Making Informed Investment Decisions

Investing in industrial property can be a lucrative venture, but it requires careful consideration and informed decision-making. To help you navigate this complex process, here are some practical steps to follow when makinginvestment decisions:

1. Conduct thorough market research: Before diving into any investment,it's crucial to understand the current state of the industrial property market.

Research factors such as vacancy rates, rental yields, and demand-supply dynamics in different locations. Look for areas with strong economic growth,infrastructure development, and a robust industrial sector.

2. Define your investment goals: Clearly

define your investment objectivesand risk tolerance. Are you looking for long-term capital appreciation or immediate rental income? Understanding your goals will help you make better decisions throughout the investment process.

3. Identify promising locations: Once you have a clear understanding of the market, identify locations that align with your investment goals. Consider factors such as proximity to transportation hubs, access to major highways, availability of skilled labor, and local regulations.

4. Evaluate potential properties: When evaluating potential properties, consider factors such as size, condition, zoning regulations, and potential for value-add opportunities. Assess the property's suitability for different types of industrial tenants and their specific requirements.

5. Analyze financials: Carefully analyze the financial aspects of each property under

consideration. Calculate projected rental income based on prevailing market rates and estimate expenses such as maintenance costs,property taxes, insurance premiums, and financing costs.

6.Seek professional advice: Engage professionals such as real estate agents or brokers who specialize in industrial properties to gain valuable insights into the local market conditions and trends. They can provide guidance on pricing negotiations and help you avoid common pitfalls.

7.Perform due diligence: Before finalizing any deal, conduct thorough due diligence on the property. This includes reviewing legal documents like leases or contracts, conducting inspections to assess the physical conditionof the property, and verifying any potential environmental or zoning issues.

8.Develop a risk management strategy: Investing in industrial property comes with inherent risks. Develop a risk management strategy that includes contingency plans for unexpected events such as tenant defaults,market downturns, or changes in regulations. Consider diversifying your portfolio to mitigate risk.

9.Network and learn from others: Networking with experienced investors and industry professionals can provide valuable insights and opportunities for collaboration. Attend industry conferences, join online forums or real estate investment groups to expand your knowledge and learn from others'experiences.

10. Continuously monitor and adapt: Once you've made an investment, it'simportant to continuously monitor the performance of your properties and stay updated on market trends. Regularly review rental rates, vacancy rates, and economic indicators to identify opportunities for optimization or adjustments to your investment strategy.

By following these practical steps, you

can make informed investment decisions in the industrial property market and increase your chances ofsuccess.

11.2 Checklists to Guide You Through the Investment Process

Investing in industrial property involves a complex process that requires careful planning and attention to detail. To help you navigate this process effectively, here are some checklists that can guide you through each stageof the investment journey:

1. Pre-Investment Checklist:

Define your investment goals and risk tolerance.

Research the industrial property market, including vacancy rates, rental yields, and demand-supply dynamics.

Identify promising locations based on economic growth, infrastructure development, and industrial sector strength. Determine your budget and financing options.

Engage professionals such as real estate agents or brokers specializing in industrial properties.

2. Property Evaluation Checklist:

Assess the suitability of potential properties based on size, condition, zoning regulations, and value-add opportunities.

Analyze financial aspects such as projected rental income, expenses (maintenance costs, taxes), financing costs.

Conduct due diligence by reviewing legal documents (leases/contracts),performing inspections, and verifying environmental/zoning issues.

3. Risk Management Checklist:

Develop a risk management strategy that includes contingency plans for tenant defaults, market downturns, or regulatory changes. Diversify your portfolio to mitigate risk. Consider insurance options to protect against unforeseen events.

4.Financing Checklist:
Explore financing options such as traditional bank loans, crowdfunding, orreal estate investment trusts (REITs).

Evaluate the terms and conditions of each financing option.

Prepare necessary documentation and meet eligibility criteria.

5.Post-Investment Checklist:
Regularly monitor the performance of your properties by reviewing rental rates, vacancy rates, and economic indicators.

Stay updated on market trends and adjust your investment strategy accordingly.

Network with experienced investors and industry professionals to gain insights and opportunities for collaboration.

By using these checklists as a guide, you can ensure that you cover all the essential aspects of the investment process and make informed decisions along the way.

Chapter 12: Conclusion and Next Steps in Industrial Property Investment

12.1 Recap of Key Concepts and Insights

In this section, we will recap the key concepts and insights discussed throughout the book on investing in industrial property. While the reference summary provides a brief overview, we will delve deeper into these conceptsto provide a comprehensive understanding.

Industrial property has gained popularity as an investment option due to its potential for high rental yields and capital appreciation. However, it is essential to understand what industrial property entails and why it is an attractive investment. Industrial properties encompass various types, Including, warehouses, distribution centers, manufacturing facilities, and logistics hubs. Each type offers unique opportunities and challenges forinvestors.

One key factor driving demand for industrial

space is the growth of e- commerce. As online shopping continues to rise, companies require more warehouse space to store inventory and fulfill orders efficiently. This trend presents an excellent opportunity for investors to capitalize on the increasing demand for industrial properties.

Another factor contributing to the attractiveness of industrial property investment is supply chain optimization. Companies are constantly seekingways to streamline their operations and reduce costs.

This often involves locating their facilities strategically near transportation hubs or major highways. Investors can benefit from this trend by identifying locations with strong transportation infrastructure that are likely to attract tenants.

Technological advancements also play a significant role in shaping theindustrial property market. Automation and robotics have revolutionized manufacturing processes, leading to increased demand for specialized facilities that can accommodate these technologies.

Investors who stay abreast of

technological trends can identify emerging opportunities in this sector.

Throughout the book, we have provided a step-by-step guide on how tonavigate the investment process successfully. From conducting thorough market research to evaluating potential properties and negotiating deals, each stage requires careful consideration and analysis.

Additionally, we have explored advanced topics such as value-add opportunities and lease negotiations. Value-add strategies involve renovating or repositioning properties to increase their income potential andattract high-quality tenants.

These strategies can significantly enhance the value of industrial properties and generate higher returns for investors.

Furthermore, we have discussed various financing options tailored specifically for industrial property investments. Traditional bank loans are a common choice, but alternative methods such as crowdfunding or real estate investment trusts (REITs) offer additional flexibility.

Understanding these financing options allows investors to choose the most suitable funding solution for their needs.

To provide practical insights, we have included real-life case studies from successful investors in the industrial property market. These stories serve as inspiration and offer valuable lessons that readers can apply to their own investment journeys. By learning from the experiences of others, investors can gain a deeper understanding of the strategies and tactics that lead to success in this asset class.

Overall, Investing in Industrial Property is not just a theoretical guide; it is a practical roadmap for success. The book provides actionable advice, checklists, and resources to help investors make informed decisions and take confident steps towards building a profitable industrial property portfolio.

12.1 Developing a Long-Term Strategy for Industrial Property Investment

In this section, we will explore how to develop a long-term strategy for industrial property investment. While the reference summary briefly mentions this topic, we will provide new insights and delve into specific areas not covered.

Developing a long-term strategy is crucial for achieving sustainable success in industrial property investment. It involves setting clear goals, identifying target markets, and formulating an investment plan that alignswith these objectives.

Firstly, it is essential to define your investment goals. Are you looking for short-term cash flow or long-term capital appreciation? Do you want to focuson acquiring properties with existing tenants or invest in value-add opportunities? Clarifying your objectives will help guide your decision- making process and ensure that your investments align with your overall strategy.

Next, identify target markets that offer favorable conditions for industrial property investment. Consider factors such as population growth, economicstability, infrastructure development, and government policies that support industrial growth. By focusing on markets with strong fundamentals, you increase the likelihood of achieving sustainable returns over the long term.

Once you have identified target markets, conduct thorough market research to gain a deep understanding of local dynamics and trends.
Analyze supply and demand factors, vacancy rates, rental yields, and potential risks. This information will inform your investment decisions and help you identify opportunities that others may overlook.

In addition to market research, it is crucial to build a network of industry professionals who can provide valuable insights and opportunities. Connect with real estate agents specializing in industrial properties, property managers, developers, and other investors. Attend industry conferences and join online forums to stay updated on the latest trends and developments in the industrial property market.

When formulating your investment plan, consider diversification as a risk management strategy. Investing in different types of industrial properties across multiple locations can mitigate the impact of localized economic downturns or shifts in tenant demand. Diversification also allows you to capitalize on various market trends and maximize your overall returns.

Furthermore, consider incorporating sustainability into your long-term strategy. The growing focus on environmental responsibility presents an opportunity for investors to differentiate their properties and attract environmentally conscious tenants. Investing in energy-efficient technologiesor incorporating green building practices can enhance the value of your portfolio while contributing to a more sustainable future.

Lastly, regularly review and adjust your long-term strategy based on changing market conditions and evolving investment goals. The industrial property market is dynamic, influenced by factors such as economic cycles,technological advancements, and regulatory changes. Staying adaptable and responsive to these changes will ensure that your strategy remains relevant and effective over time.

12.2 Taking Confident Steps towards Building a Profitable Portfolio

In this section, we will explore how investors can take confident steps towards building a profitable industrial property portfolio. While the reference summary briefly mentions this topic, we will provide new insights by delving into specific areas not covered.

Building a profitable portfolio requires careful planning, diligent execution,and continuous evaluation. Here are some key steps to consider:

1.Start with a solid foundation: Before diving into property acquisitions, ensure that you have a strong financial foundation. Establish a clear budget,assess your risk tolerance, and secure appropriate financing options. Having a solid financial base will provide the confidence and stability needed to navigate the investment process.

2.Conduct thorough due diligence: When evaluating potential properties,conduct comprehensive due diligence to assess their suitability for investment. This includes analyzing financial statements, reviewing lease agreements, inspecting the physical condition of the property, and assessing market demand. Thorough due diligence minimizes the risk of unforeseen issues and ensures that you make informed investment decisions.

3. Seek professional advice: Engage professionals such as real estate agents, lawyers, accountants, and property managers who specialize in industrial property investments. Their expertise can help you navigate complex legal and financial matters while providing valuable insights into market trends and opportunities.

4. Develop relationships with industry stakeholders: Building relationships with key industry stakeholders can open doors to new opportunities and provide access to off-market deals. Attend networking events, join industry associations, and actively engage with professionals in the industrial property sector.

5. Implement effective property management strategies: Effective property management is crucial for maximizing returns on your investments. Ensure that your properties are well-maintained, respond

promptly to tenant needs,and regularly review rental rates to stay competitive in the market.

6.Continuously monitor market conditions: Stay informed about market trends by monitoring economic indicators, vacancy rates, rental yields, and regulatory changes that may impact industrial property investments.
Regularly evaluate your portfolio's performance against these factors to identify areas for improvement or potential risks.

7.Embrace technology: Leverage technology tools such as data analytics platforms or property management software to streamline operations and enhance decision-making processes. Technology can provide valuable insights into tenant preferences, market trends, and property performance,enabling you to make data-driven investment decisions.

8. Consider partnerships or joint ventures:
Collaborating with other investors through partnerships or joint ventures can provide access to larger-scale projects and diversify risk. Pooling resources and expertise canlead to more significant opportunities and shared success.

9. Stay disciplined and patient: Building a profitable industrial propertyportfolio takes time and requires discipline. Avoid making impulsive investment decisions based on short-term market fluctuations. Instead,focus on your long-term strategy and be patient in waiting for the right opportunities that align with your investment goals.

By following these steps, investors can take confident strides towards building a profitable industrial property portfolio. Remember that success in this asset class requires a combination of knowledge, experience, and adaptability. Continuously educate yourself about the market, learn from industry experts, and stay committed to your long-term strategy. With perseverance and careful planning, investing in industrial property can provide lucrative returns and long-term financial stability.

Acknowledgements

- "Industrial Property Investment: Strategies and Best Practices" by David Lynn

- "The Handbook of Industrial Property Investing" by Richard Reed

- "Investing in Industrial Properties: A Guide for Real Estate Investors" by Brian Hennessey

- "Industrial Real Estate Investment: A Comprehensive Guide to Understanding the Risks and Rewards" by Michael J. Meeks and Howard K.Samuels

- "The Impact of E-commerce on Industrial Real Estate by JLL

- "Supply Chain Optimization and the Role of Industrial Real Estate" by CBRE

- "Technological Advancements in

Industrial Real Estate" by Colliers International

- "Industrial Property Investment: A Comprehensive Guide" by Richard M. Betts
- "Market Research for Real Estate: A Guide to Understanding and Analyzing the Commercial Property Market" by Richard Reed
- "The Handbook of Industrial Property Investment: Strategies for Success" by David G. Jones
- "Real Estate Market Analysis: Methods and Case Studies "by Deborah L. Brett and Adrienne Schmitz
- "The Due Diligence Handbook For Commercial Real Estate: A Proven
- System To Save Time, Money, Headaches And Create Value When Buying Commercial Real Estate" by Brian Hennessey
- "Commercial Real Estate Investing: A Creative Guide to

Successfully Making Money" by
Dolf de Roos

- "The Art of Negotiation in Business and
  Life" by Michael Wheeler
- "Industrial Property Renovation:
  Strategies for Success" by Michael Bull
- "Repositioning Industrial Properties:
  Strategies for Success" by Richard
  Wilson
- "Attracting High-Quality Tenants in
  Industrial Real Estate" by John McNellis
- "The Value-Add Playbook: How
  to Create Extraordinary Value in
  Industrial Real Estate" by Gary
  Nussbaum
- "Industrial Property Development:
  A Guide to Successful
  Redevelopment "by Richard F.
  Wilson
- "Redevelopment:Opportunities
  and Challenges" by David
  Listokin
- "Urban Redevelopment: A Handbook for
  Real Estate Professionals" by Harris M.

- "Commercial Real Estate Leases: Understanding the Basics" by NAIOP (National Association of Industrial and Office Properties)
- "The Art of Negotiating Commercial Real Estate Leases" by DLA Piper
- "Managing Industrial Property Tenants: Best Practices for Success" byBOMA International (Building Owners and Managers Association)
- "Lease Renewal Strategies for Commercial Real Estate Investors" by CCIM Institute (Certified Commercial Investment Member)
- "Effective Tenant Relationship Management in Industrial Property Investments" by Urban Land Institute
- "Real Estate Investment Trusts: Structure, Performance, and Investment Opportunities" by John McMahan
- "The Handbook of Real Estate Investment Trusts" by Joseph L. Pagliari Jr., Richard T. Monopoli, and James R.

DeLisle

- "Investing in REITs: Real Estate Investment Trusts" by Ralph L. Block

- "The Intelligent REIT Investor: How to Build Wealth with Real EstateInvestment Trusts" by Stephanie Krewson-Kelly and R. Brad Thomas

- "The Complete Guide to Buying and Selling Industrial Property" by Bob Copperfield

- "Commercial Real Estate Investing: A Creative Guide to Successfully Making Money" by Dolf de Roos

- "The Intelligent REIT Investor: How to Build Wealth with Real Estate Investment Trusts" by Stephanie Krewson-Kelly and R. Brad Thomas

- "The Handbook of Commercial Real Estate Investing" by John McMahan

- "Investing in Industrial Property: A Comprehensive Guide"

- "The Complete Guide to Real Estate

Finance for Investment Properties"by Steve Berges

- "The Handbook of Commercial Real Estate Investing" by JohnMcMahan
- "Industrial Real Estate: Understanding the Investment Landscape" by David Lynn
- "Investing in Industrial Property: A Guide for Beginners" by Mark Ferguson
- "Industrial Property Investment: Strategies for Success" by Richard Reed